Praise for
BABY SUGGS AND A PURPLE BUTTERFLY

Baby Suggs and a Purple Butterfly is a stunning and unique guided journal and poetry anthology. We are told this book is "a collection of sermons, spells, codes and letters from various women of color from all walks of life, their stories reveal the various ways we are still holy despite life's traumas and heartbreaks." The intro invites the reader to enter a sacred space where our voices and our stories are invited to come along on a magical journey. Indeed, after reading these spirited pieces we become a part of their sacred spaces and their memories. Each contributor gifts us a writing prompt, an invitation to be in conversation and creative community with these talented writers. Poet Kim Brandon's prompt invites the reader to join on a healing journey: "Crying and laughter are both medicines for our pain. They remind us of how much we carry in us, how much we can feel. …How has both been a part of your healing journey? How has both been a part of your being?" Poet .chisaraokwu's vivid imagery mesmerizes us: "she wants to shut up / her womb with keloids / & till her skin / ' til it ' s dirt thin wet." .chisaraokwu's prompt explains how her poem explores myths/narratives/ and stories of ancestors whose DNA sits in our bones and invites us to "Let the ancestors in your house breathe." This poet's prompt instructs us to take a deep collective healing exhale. Poet LeConté Dill explains how to write a Golden Shovel poem and invites the reader to borrow from another "poem, song, novel, play, speech, or film" as we see fit. Poems in this anthology are instructive, are in conversation with each other, and are an invitation for the reader to be in creative community with both the poems and their poets. Jacqueline Carr's prompt expands our possibilities: "Receptivity opens us up for many possibilities. It shows us the multitude of who we are. Write about how you are a receptacle and what you are receiving on your personal journeys."

This is a remarkable collection that the reader will continue to revisit, re-read and thanks to the novel guided journal format, create bold new work using creative prompts that are gifted to us.

—JP Howard, author of *SAY/MIRROR*

Baby Suggs and a Purple Butterfly is a book that shimmers with the sounds of tenderness. Sherese Francis has gathered some of our most courageous voices here in these pages filled with breaking, mending, refusal, celebration and hope. This book is a sacred space, a path, a clearing. The prompts after each piece are invitations to embark on our own writing journeys, but they are also profound urgings toward deeper and richer living. I am grateful for this bouquet of light.

—Mariahadessa Ekere Tallie, author of
The Unwieldy Otherwise: Rethinking the Roots of Performance Studies in and through the Black Freedom Struggle, her first academic publication, co-authored with Leon Hilton published in *Performance Matters*

Baby Suggs

AND A

Purple Butterfly

EDITED BY

Sherese Francis

Copyright © 2024 by Sherese Francis

All rights reserved. No part of this book may be reproduced in any manner without written consent except for the quotation of short passages used inside of an article, criticism, or review.

Get Fresh Publishing, A Non-Profit Corp.
PO Box 901
Union, NJ 07083

www.gfbpublishing.org

ISBN: 9798218417741

Library of Congress Control Number: 2024937843

Cover, layout, typesetting, and design:
culture glut llc
cultureglut.com

This book was typeset in Mrs. Eaves & Bembo Std.

Table of Contents

Introduction *by Sherese Francis*..1

SERMONS —

For Baby Suggs—May I laugh too? *by Kim D. Brandon*.....................7
Prompt *by Sherese Francis*..9
In the House of the Ancestors *by .CHISARAOKWU*......................10
Prompt *by .chisaraokwu*...13
Freedom *by Jacqueline Johnson*...15
Prompt *by Sherese Francis*..18
The Day I Woke Up with Mud Under My Nails *by Divya Kandwal*........20
Prompt *by Sherese Francis*..22
Libations *by Kuukua Dzigbordi Yomekpe*......................................24
Prompts *by Kuukua Dzigbordi Yomekpe*......................................26
I Wish We Had More Time *by Jacqueline Carr*..............................28
Prompt *by Sherese Francis*..29
Patchwork Woman *by Divya Kandwal*..31
Prompt *by Sherese Francis*..34
Homily on High *by Carla Cherry*...36
Prompt *by Sherese Francis*..40

SPELLS —

new tendernesses *by blkcowrie* 45
Prompt *by Sherese Francis* 46
Mettle *by Carla Cherry* 48
Prompt *by Sherese Francis* 50
Receiver *by Jacqueline Johnson* 52
Prompt *by Sherese Francis* 53
Gather *by Kim D. Brandon* 55
Prompt *by Sherese Francis* 58
enter the circle *by blkcowrie* 60
Prompt *by Sherese Francis* 66

CODES —

Define you? *by Zahura Akter* 71
Prompt *by Sherese Francis* 73
Taboo Women *by Sherese Francis* 75
Prompt *by Sherese Francis* 76
Helping to Understand! *by Zahura Akter* 78
Prompt *by Sherese Francis* 79
When I Come Back *by .CHISARAOKWU.* 81
Prompt *by .CHISARAOKWU.* 82

LETTERS —

    after Lucille Clifton's "come celebrate with me" *blkcowrie* 87
    Prompt *by Sherese Francis* 89
    Relay Racing *by Kim D. Brandon* 91
    Prompt *by Sherese Francis* 94
    What I Leave Behind? *by Jacqueline Carr* 96
    Prompt *by Sherese Francis* 97
    What Would I Take? *by Jacqueline Carr* 99
    Prompt *by Sherese Francis* 100
    Finding My Way *by LeConté Dill* 102
    Prompt *by LeConté Dill* 103
    Poor Dear *by Keisha-Gaye Anderson* 105
    Prompt *by Sherese Francis* 107

    Acknowledgements 111
    Bios 113

Introduction

Baby Suggs, holy, was starved for color. She spent years feeding a Black congregation in the Clearing, reminding them of their own light. Then one day a shadow came over her and her great heart broke, but in her heart breaking, she was able to see a range of colors and all their meanings. To find another articulation for all that was in her.

Baby Suggs, holy, a name she chose for herself because it meant someone loved her, someone claimed her, there was someone to whom she always belonged. Her name—a birthing of abundance, power, creativity, and song.

Baby Suggs, holy, who robed herself, anointed herself, gave herself a throne, gave herself a staff of power, cleared a sacred space for herself and others with her own words.

Baby Suggs, holy, who told her congregation to celebrate in the ceremony of life—to dance, to laugh, to cry, to touch each other deeply. That the grace they sought was in their imaginations. That they had the power to imagine their own grace.

Baby Suggs, holy, whose faith was tested by Sethe's arrival and who was forced to see shades and colors she had not witnessed before. Sethe who found rest, comfort, and love in Baby Suggs, even as Sethe struggled to see her own holiness.

Baby Suggs, holy, in her revelations, revealed that in the dark earth of our bodies, gathered are the roots of ourselves, and in those roots are many seeds, branches, stars, and colors. We are our own sacred text, written in our flesh. We are our own breakthroughs. We are our own best thing. Because we are here and that is enough. In our roots are our crowns, is the pink headstone to remember the little girls we thought lost within us, are the white flowers and dark-red-to-purple fruit of our brown chokecherry trees, is the butterfly coming out of the cocoon, are our records of transformation, is our healing. Love them all hard.

Enwrap yourself with a carnival quilt of all the possibilities of colors. With your ability to craft your own art of self, your own stories.

Baby Suggs, holy.

In this collection of sermons, spells, codes, and letters from various women of color from all walks of life, our stories reveal the various ways we are still holy despite life's traumas and heartbreaks. The ways we name ourselves as a way to claim ourselves. The ways we acknowledge our dynamic power and light within us. The ways our stories bring us together. The ways our stories show us those rare glimpses into the wholeness of the divine. The ways our stories reveal all the possibilities of love within us. The ways our stories that we leave behind become sacred spaces for others. We carry so much memory within our bodies and from those memories, we can blossom; we can find flight.

"White and purple with a tender tail and a hard head carrots and turnips. Feels good when you hold it in your hand and smells like the creek when it floods, bitter but happy. We'll smell them together. Beloved. Beloved. Because you mine and I have to show you these things, and teach you what a mother should. Funny how you lose sight of somethings and memory others." –Toni Morrison.

In this collection full of sacred texts, there is also space for you, as the reader, to share your own texts in this larger chorus. Your voice and your stories are here to join with the others.

SERMONS

For Baby Suggs—May I laugh too?
by Kim D. Brandon

There was before
And now there is only this right here
I was somebody's somebody once

Always before I know it
A feelin' so strong
Come on me

Like they gonna call me
By my name and I'm
Goin' whip around
And remember, see them
Rememberin' them
Rememberin' me
Rememberin' a place
Rememberin' a time
Rememberin' a smell
A full stomach
A soft mat on the floor

I'm gonna remember
All that came in the before
Before
Being stolen, ripped apart
Left for dead

So when Baby Suggs says
For us women to weep
I was already weepin'
Low like
Deeper than all that wailin'

That mornin'
I wished somehow she says
For us women to laugh
Loud, laugh until my belly
Shook like blueberry jam

Cause I got me this feelin' see
I got me this feelin'
Laughin' might sound like my name
And
If I heard my name
Maybe I would
Remember the before
Who I belonged to
Once when I belonged to
A mama or
Somebody
Somebody special

Prompt
by Sherese Francis

Crying and laughter are both medicines for our pain. They remind us of how much we carry in us, how much we can feel. What do you choose to remember? What has made you cry? What has brought you laughter? How have both been a part of your healing journey? How have both been a part of your being?

In the House of the Ancestors
by .CHISARAOKWU.

*(Or My Skin is Soft-haired Doorway
into Tiny Homes Where Crescent-moon People
Wash Clothing in Milky Dreams & Rising Suns)*

i.

before
i lived here
there were others
shaped like callouses
treading the earth softly—
their women's necks dressed
in orange beads & red-coifed
men chewing sticks in their mouths.
in their mouths they began to dream.

ii.

with each heart-
beat the conquistadores
in red hats rediscovered
another me forgetting they had already
tilled & reaped—today they will
graze upon the unshaven parts
with rough tongues
& blunt teeth

& i will spill my milk
at their feet where they sliced
my fruit until I bled
their efforts on the ground.

iii.

she wants to shut up
her womb with keloids
& till her skin
'til it's dirt-thin wet—
a sober field of dreams
she won't regret,
but
if she does the earth will
not make room for her
& all the hers that will
inhabit her. the future,
the future must be
star bright.

iv.

yesterday, the conquistadores
crushed an anthill
in the middle of a field
oozing honey   bees
gathered in memoriam,
laying flowers on graves
of ants who dared to die.
the ant is not the enemy

but a star in the night
sky. the bees understand this
& bow   man will find
other fears to justify his nature.

v.

the moon people smile
with large white teeth &
dimpled cheeks sipping
coconut juice & palm wine on the eve
of each solstice. i feel
their laugh when the earth shakes.
it is then that I remember them
as they were before the sun set.

Prompt
by .chisaraokwu.

This poem explores the myths/narratives/stories of the ancestors whose DNA sits in our bones, literally and figuratively. The speaker comes from West Africa, has ancestors with and without sickle cell, ancestors who lived in the old world and the new world, scattered in the oceans, smiling through the eyes of their descendants. In your own work, generating space, consider your own body and what it represents of your ancestry—each hair on your head, the way your fingers curve or your toes lay. Are there chronic conditions, certain physical features, skills, or other traits that you have in common with your ancestors? Perhaps, take a look at old family photos, and see if something emerges. On the other hand, is something missing from the narrative? Are your flesh and bone in solitude, in isolation, an island unto themselves due to circumstances of lineage and ancestry? What might that feel like in the body—a body that houses all this information that can't be decoded, or isn't easily deciphered? Take some time to consider how your body houses the ancestors, the elders, the stories of your people. What are they trying to tell you? What can you do with this body in this moment that maybe they could not? Whatever it is, make it yours. Let the ancestors in your house breathe.

Freedom

by Jacqueline Johnson

I.

Not two seconds out of that wagon,
and I know one thing – I'm free.
I own me. I own this body,
these deep brown arms and wide hips.
And I own my legs, broke down as they are.
They're mine. Bless my legs.
I ain't never seen my face. I own it too.

Bless my name. Mrs. Baby Suggs.

Damn master Garner. Work for him over
ten years, and he still don't know my real name.
My name is Baby. Mrs. Baby Suggs. Not Jenny.
Not Jenny Whitlow. Baby. Baby Suggs is my name.
My husband's name. The one that run away.
Henry Suggs, one I'm looking for now.

II.

There are many ways of knowing.
My way of knowing was to listen to the heavens.
Observe the shifts in scent in the wind.
The way a bough shimmered in noonday sun.
The messages came through air.
Allowed me to see what's coming.
May not always call it by name.

That morning, nothing I did came out right.
Curdled eggs in my pudding.
Two dead baby hogs in the yard.
The meanest energy among the newly freed was
so thick, I could barely see anything clearly.
How you gonna get past an anger a hundred years deep?
An anger erupting at the first sign of joy.
Tried over and over. I could not clear the darkness.

Just a few minutes' warning from the ones on the road
woulda saved Sethe and that baby,
boys and all.
Used to be folks had each other's backs.
Not these county-city negroes. Let envy be they everlasting god.
They come to my house, eat up all my food.
Don't even have even a gesture of kindness.
Not a one.

Stamp Paid and I was gazing upon the waters instead of the land
in its near holy greenness.
Looking for a sign, any sign, when
those slavers came looking for Sethe.
Maggot men.
So sure of themselves, had a wagon and a gun.

III.

Damn Sethe.
How she gonna try and kill all my grandbabies.
How she try and kill all my futures.
How she gonna kill all Halle's futures.

Sethe cut four. I saved three.
I couldn't save the baby girl.
Sethe carry the last one in her womb with her to jail.
I don't know if we will ever get that one back.

Prompt
by Sherese Francis

The story of Margaret Garner inspired Toni Morrison to write *Beloved*. The larger historical horrors of slavery impacted the personal decisions of Garner. Select a figure or archetype from the past or from contemporary times. It could be someone well-known or someone who is hidden or anonymous. Choose or create either a moment of crisis or change in their life and use that moment to tell something larger or deeper about them and the historical moment that shapes their choices.

The Day I Woke Up with Mud Under My Nails
by Divya Kandwal

On the day that I woke up with mud under my nails,
The summer sun was burning.
Punishing, purifying, purging
The lingering stench of a moonless night.
My grandmother was offering water
To Surya, the Sun God.

A ritual, I've never been sure
If she believed in
Or merely carried out
Because it is expected.
A duty, a life sentence meant to outlive her
And me.

On the day that I woke up with mud under my nails
The summer sun was burning.
I left the house with my bag
Overflowing with angst, fear, and lack.
I sat in my therapist's office, waiting,
Nodding, sighing, thinking.

You see, the problem is
My face is not my own.
I always feel like I'm dreaming.
For months, I've been slicing these fingers,
Hunting for pain, for a throbbing
Nerve. Something.

The day I woke up with mud under my nails,
The summer sun was burning.
The air was heavy, clogged, waxy
with the sweet smell of rotting mangoes
hanging desperately by frayed stems.
A fall could mean freedom or the end.

Living in a house of wallpaper women,
I've been taught the art of shoveling,
Burying blasphemous thoughts, acidic feelings
Under layers and layers of scabbed skin.
At night, in secret, I scratch and slash and slit
My flesh, to peek at the maggots that live within.

My legacy is that of repression,
Of burying and carefully cultivating
An exterior too polished to match the interior.
But I fail at apathy,
My appetite, too voracious, engulfing,
Swallowing stories of subversive women saving galaxies.

On the day I woke up with mud under my nails,
The summer sun was burning.
Tiny plants were growing on my papery skin,
pushing through the cracks and slits.
but instead of wrenching out the roots, digging
Today, I let them live.

Prompt
by Sherese Francis

Create your own ritual of unburying through the use of a refrain. What day did you decide to stop burying your truths and instead come up from the dirt? What learned routines and habits from your family did you decide to leave behind? What inside of you did you decide to let live? What did it feel like?

Libations
by Kuukua Dzigbordi Yomekpe

My sister got married today.
She asked me to pour the ceremonial libation,
An integral part of any auspicious gathering in our Ghanaian culture.

I positioned myself and steadied the plant that would be the recipient.
My voice and hands shook as
I juggled the mic and my calabash full of water.

I poured the first offering.
I paused.
I thought of Dad, who went to rest in 2003.
I thought of Mom, who made the choice not to be at her daughter's wedding.
I thought of aunts and uncles who have succumbed to cancer,
Who would have been there shaking a leg.
I thought of the woman who raised my sister and me,
My maternal grandmother,
How we no longer speak.

In the calabash, the water swirled with the wounds of yesteryear,
Wounds that have scabbed over but have not fully healed,
Wounds from Ghana,
Wounds from the twenty-three years since we immigrated
To this here land of milk and honey,
Wounds that will start to bleed afresh
If anyone picks at the scabs above them.

Today, when I poured libation,
A sob escaped my soul and ran free.
I worried that the dear brethren, dearly beloved,
Gathered to celebrate such a joyous occasion,
Might mistake it for sadness, or worse, jealousy.
The sob stirred tears, but
I didn't want to ruin my makeup or the bride's,
So resolved,
I continued uttering the ceremonial incantations,
Keeping the tears at bay.
The last pour of the ceremonial water
Found me teetering on the edge –
I quickly hugged the bride,
Holding her a second longer than usual,
Hugged my newly minted brother-in-law, and
Returned to my dinner table promptly before I lost my steely resolve.

Only I had already picked at the scabs, and
The wounds, though ages old,
Bleed afresh tonight.

Prompt
by Kuukua Dzigbordi Yomekpe

Write about a tradition or custom that is performed at family gatherings. It can be formal, ceremonial, ritualistic, or simply something y'all just do and call it tradition.

What images do weddings and marriage ceremonies conjure up for you? What is your relation to these images? What do you do when you encounter these images?

Scabs. The word comes with a built-in connotation. Ugly, painful, before scars, scabs must form. Write about your relationship to scabs. Do they gross you out, intrigue you? Do you pick at them? Cover them? Smother them in shea or cocoa butter and hope for the best?

I Wish We Had More Time
by Jacqueline Carr

Death and dying—hard realities we all must face. There is no escaping; one day it will happen to us, our parents, our friends, our enemies, our siblings — no one is spared.

Glen was nearing his expiration date. He became confined to his bed and was in a child-like state; watching him suffer and deteriorate broke my heart into pieces. I visited him regularly; and when I did, I felt a sadness so bracing I had to look away to avoid direct eye contact for fear that he would see the tears in my eyes. Alone, I questioned God and his existence– why was he allowing this to happen to such a good person?

I saw a glimmer of joy in his eyes whenever I reminded him of stories of our past and the risks we took when we were younger. I saw the effort as well as the pain it took for him to smile, a smile that was seemingly strained, and resigned. I sensed that he probably knew that his days were numbered and that it was just a matter of time.

My heart wept for him as I prayed for God's mercy and grace upon his soul; I wished he was in better health so that we could spend a little more time to do the things we enjoyed, such as watching the sunset, going on long road trips, and talking about places to visit on our bucket lists.

I hated that his breathing was labored. As I watched him lying there, I felt guilty but didn't know why. I grappled with the notion of life's fragility as I realized that reality finally caught up with my denial about his ultimate demise. I wondered about this thing called "life," knowing that it's both joyful and sorrowful, wrapped in a vacuum that I can't begin to fathom.

I got tired of shaking my head in disbelief and resignation. I got tired of watching him waste away and wishing that he could eat solid food. Why, dear God, must it be this way? Why must some of us suffer so much before transitioning? I had a ton of questions for God for which I received no satisfactory answers.

All I wanted and prayed for was for God to give us a little more time together.

Prompt
by Sherese Francis

To watch a loved one suffer in their state of transition is painful to endure. We can feel the ache through our bodies. It stirs within us the memories we share with them and the future memories we will lose. It stirs within us thoughts of our own life and mortality. Write about grief as a work of witness. What stories lay within your time of grief? How does grief bring us into conversation with the divine, to question our own lives, to cherish what we still have?

Patchwork Woman
by Divya Kandwal

Sit here.
Breathe deep, pause, and
Tell me,
Tell me
Your ghastly secrets,
Clandestine thoughts,
The blasphemy –
Tell me.

Listening is passive, and
I, an authority of passivity.
Every word formed by your lips,
Every notion, every belief –
I'll smother them with cotton
And wrap them with twine.
Yours words are now mine.

I'm your friend, a companion.
I'll offer you comfort,
Soothe your ego,
Batter your hurt –
But first
Tell me,
Tell me
Secrets crackling against your flesh,
Forging out from the cracks in your skin,
Murmurings of sacrilege,
Of acrimony and the hatred within.

I'll nod and shoot
An empathetic glance.
I'll reassure you
Of your tender sainthood,
And then
I'll dance.
I'll dance.

Your fears, your thoughts,
The sigh of despair
Before you paused,
Blinked once, twice,
Three times –
Are all mine.

I am man.
An animated mosaic
Of purloined peculiarities.
I frolic and forage
For victims to fool,
Then engulf and consume.

With borrowed delicate fingers,
I unwrap the twine,
Preserve the cotton for the next time, and
Gorge myself on gestures
Hitherto yours, now mine.

Am I an experiment or a scientist?
Call me Doctor Frankenstein.

After class, I'm stopped by a boy
Who praises me for my
Idiosyncratic style.
I notice his dainty shrug.
I smirk,
Then smile.

Prompt
by Sherese Francis

Dig a little deeper. How do you weave together all the stories of yourself and others—the beautiful, the good, the ugly, and the bad? How do you find a way to still love them and still find joy or power in them? Write a mythic poem about a character who is a fusion of all the parts of who you are.

Homily on High
by Carla Cherry

Around finals one year, a few of us gathered around a table
with Dr. Gloria Wade-Gayles, and she admonished:
You're not tired. Your mothers are tired.

Had I paid her the same heed as
ozone in my nostrils,
fat drops of rain on my face urging me indoors,
I'd have plunged to my knees, cried,
Hallelujah!
Amen!
the day my mother, who did not have
a room of her own until she was sixty-two, announced:
I just want to be still
and be quiet.

We had come for her,
survivor of a gambling father
who drank too much to keep them in one home,
social worker who tried to
pry her and her four brothers apart from their mother.
Her teachers refused to let this
intellectually gifted Black girl
who loved to read,
skip a grade.
A secretarial job at MetLife
to help lift the family off welfare,
but Mom still had to share a bed with Grandma
until she married Daddy at twenty-nine.

Nights looking out the windows of their South Bronx apartment
as sirens wailed,
scared Daddy wouldn't make it home
after thugs threatened him with a knife
at the school across the street where he volunteered.

Birthed two daughters, cooked almost every night for four,
inhaled Comet or Mr. Clean as she scrubbed
the bathroom floors and the bathtub on her knees,
sewed, mended, ironed clothes for us, for herself,
knitted afghans to warm us through winter naps,
washed, blow-dried, braided or pressed three heads of hair,
squeezed her bosom into a bra
that left dents in her shoulders and
answered to her first name from Dr. and Mister So-and-So
when Daddy couldn't make it work on one income.

Then the day she heard the pop—
She called home gasping for Daddy.
Uncle Don had shot himself in his bedroom.
She got Grandma out of Queensbridge.
Uncle Ralph died five years later from a stroke.
Uncle Reggie, four years after that.
Ran through her paychecks to help Daddy
put my sister and me through college.

And then I, at twenty-two, was clung to her hands
as I was laid out on a cold metal table,
cursing the hot rip of my flesh,
then pacing the floor,
my son squalling against my shoulder,

me, wondering what he could drink that wouldn't make him sick
when my milk wasn't enough,
imploring, How do I do this?
You just have to dig deep and find the strength.

Two years later, she nursed Grandma through her liver cancer,
my sister also needed before and after work care for her daughter,
so Mommy fed her grandbabies pancakes drizzled with real maple syrup at breakfast,
fed them snacks, and kept them safe and clean after school
until we got home from work.

Daddy, because busy Black women impressed him most,
urged her to join a book club at church,
go to college for the degree her high school guidance counselor
told her she couldn't get because she was a Negro.

Neighbors,
covetous of her nimble-fingered choreography—home keys and back—
shorthand, and perfect grammar,
invited her to join committees and take their notes.

I shouldn't have been surprised by Mommy reclaiming her time.

That birthmark above her navel looks like a fish.

As I live through my own series of struggles
that now make me close my eyes at church,
rock, and weep
when the choir sings,
I sometimes mimic
the tulip,
crocus,
poppy,
hibiscus,
as they close their petals at night.
I thank my mother for the lesson.
Hallelujah.
Amen.

Prompt
by Sherese Francis

Write about the generational stories passed down to you that shaped your own story. What lessons have you learned from elders and ancestors in your life about striving to reclaim your time and space for yourself? How did they teach you to see yourself as holy and worthy of rest too? What praise songs would you write for these lessons given to you?

SPELLS

—

new tenderness
by blkcowrie

    every year every winter
    melanin crowds my mouth
        abundant with Blacknesses
                reaching my lips

        what is no longer useful
        dries & fades & flakes

            eventually

                    oatmeal shea cocoa butter
                  coconut oil castor oil aloe
                attempt rescue
            bits of earth
            butter up new tendernesses
            eager to
                take
                    your place
                          beside
                  this *slick*
                smile
            atop chin
            even inside dimpled cradles
            of this kiss
              every year every ancestor
                refuels my melanin
                  protects my cosmology

        as i soften my stem
            with spring

Prompt
by Sherese Francis

Audre Lorde told us about the power of the erotic, in living deeply full lives. During the winter of our lives is a time to go inward and tend to the parts of ourselves that need care. Write about the ways you give yourself care. Where on your body can you give more of your attention? How can you show yourself more tenderness? How does tenderness connect you more deeply to your true natures? How does tenderness bring you into a new spring in your lives?

Mettle
by Carla Cherry

Grandmother knew
rune and roots,
taught me to forge
home into halidom,
beyond soapy water on
skin,
floors,
walls.

I asked her to teach me magic.
She made me drink
a cup of dill tea every night.
It's good for your ears.
You will even hear
music in the rhythm of your own feet.

She had me
rub lemon/salt/ammonia/water
on doorknobs.

She showed me how to hold an egg
in the plume of smoke
of burning frankincense,
and with the egg in
in my right hand,
pass it over the crown of my head,
my eyes,
nose,
lips,
neck,
shoulders,
solar plexus,
knees,
toes.
Daub my skin with sandalwood
from toes to crown,
sealing aura.

Candlelit meditation.

Prompt
by Sherese Francis

We have an entire community of nature that supports our resiliency. Write about some of the medicines and rituals that you learned from an elder that continue to support your resilient spirit. How have these medicines and rituals helped you forge your own sacred space?

Receiver

by Jacqueline Johnson

Big woman from Lorain.
Keeper of signs, whoops, and wails.
How fitting you bleed our history
onto reams of paper.

Receiver for Sula, First Corinthians, Pilate,
Guitar, Sethe, Paul D, and Beloved.
So many times, I saw you in Manhattan.
Your gaze always curious to see the folk.

How your golden language lives in us.
Old queen with silver dreads to valley
and center of your back. Used to be a
homespun woman mixing,

alchemy of spirit, and words to see who
we might yet become under your pen.

Prompt
by Sherese Francis

The preservation of sacred knowledges and traditions rely on the passing down and receiving of them through time and space. What technologies (language, rituals, devices, objects) would you create to help in the survival of those knowledges and traditions?

Gather
by Kim D. Brandon

Gather in the circle
Gather hearts on high
One by two
Two by four

Let the crimes of those allowed to be
And came when called "master"
Fall from your skin like rain at harvest
Let the crimes of those who have temporary power
Shake off your backs like fleas and dust mites

Let the love of Mother Africa gather up her heirs, her children
Let her eyes fill until the sight
And vision of future generations are restored

Let the power of Mother Africa
Call her children to recall, to remember
Theirs is a mighty culture beyond the laws of those
Who wear starch white shirts but stink of greed and terror

Let the light of Mother Africa plant seeds of vision
Let it lock our hands and hearts in the struggle for liberty
Let us be the people who cannot be separated by the whip, the gun, or the dollar
Let us gather on land too precious to be bartered

Let us be the people who come from many tribes to create a bond
That shatters fear
Let us be the people who come upon each other with open hands
Sharing what is on the table, filling the bellies and souls of barefoot armies

Let us know that we are the people
We are the people
Though the ages where life started
And here in the demand to restore liberty
We are the first
The light in heaven's windows
Even in the darkest days
Not at the hand of cowards, criminals, rapists, murderers, and thieves
The light refuses to go out

The light of humanity glows in the soul of the Nubian people
The gatekeepers to all things holy

So gather, gather one and all
Gather and let the children watch
As the soul of a people
The hearts of the world's gatekeepers
Hand in hand
Arm in arm
Heart to heart
Open up the gates between the living and the dead
The living and the not yet born
The not yet born and the ancestors
Let the light beams bounce off each other
In the here now and the here after
Until drums sing and bare feet dance
And libations are poured
Connections are made
That shore up the Nubian people
Until the end of time and beyond

Gather in the name of gatekeepers
Gather in the light of the soul
Gather

Prompt
by Sherese Francis

A sacred space is one where we can place and protect all we value the most from the oppressive forces outside attempting to destroy them. Creating a sacred space is a purposeful act and requires a continuous practice of engaging, affirming, and remembering. Write a piece gathering all you value into a sacred space, affirming the presence of each with your words.

enter the circle
by blkcowrie

you see a ring of salt
we say
'tis the ocean that holds our ancestors
between no-more-home   ★ & ★
never-will-be-home
so much more suitable
than the hulls of ships stealing our bones
you will be safe here
ocean is the only place left unchained
its wildness holds our freedom
it will protect you

you see a pentagram
a pentacle—a star, encircled by sun
we say
'tis a tribute to the open, toothy grins
of sharks
who swallow our bodies whole
when tossed to them like chum   toothy
like your grinnin' pals   toothy
with promises they *swear*
can only be found
in the core of their bellies
it reminds us
to seek earth, to seek grounding
it reminds us
when we seek to reach for currency

in these currents instead of each other
choosing to chase shiny coins
& lo(o)se change
  tossed into concrete fountains
     purporting to hold
   our dreams
the only wishes granted
churn you in their guts
incarcerate you in their ribs
they gulp your very blood
it reminds us
placing pyramid schemes
above the value of one's soul
only entombs us all
in the end

humbly now, you ask:
are those moon crescents opposite each other
slivers in mirror?

we say
you are indeed growing wiser
'tis mama moon who greets us
when we swim by night to unsafe shores
as orishas tease tides, as we gulp for air
mama moon gentles them for our passage
encircling our earthen selves against
scorches of sun
holding the vast immensity of hearts
true in her cups
when oceans too flimsy to carry our joy

our dreams, our memories, our love
& their betrayals
into this cup
you can pour your question
the other will pour out your answer
focus your mind while opening it
for that is the only way one can hold
the pattern of the eternal present
in this human life

discombobulated, assumptions shuffled
you become worried at the sight of swords
& see blades long with lethality
we say
shhhhhhh…
focus your mind.
for far-reaching dreams to reach
they must be carried by air
don't you remember the feathered spears
whose pierces fed you? arrows
protecting your villages, your homes, your beloveds
against the insistence of other arrows?? bleeding you
to the bone if you ignored their power??? mesmerized
by their winking glints flying like birds on the wind
in the rancid air?! focus your mind
lest it kill you
for it is always better to be
on this edge of the machete
than the other

awed, you ask:
is this magic?

we say
reach out with your left hand
& cut the deck from the "right" to
the left
for that is truly the righteous direction
we will take this pile of whispers
one portion at a time
always moving our expectations
our hopes, our fears, our visions to
the left, to reorganize, again
our warmth, our love, our unquenchable starlight
shall be ready to receive
having learned the folly of our arrogance
of our traitorous beliefs
that we can direct the universe
that we can chain nature to
our will
instead of just our selves to
each other
we shall glow melanin with wisdoms
harmonious with life's flickering dance
if only for these brief moments
of flesh
before we are returned to the eternal ether
free of the confines of limitation
yet still humming with the memory
of beauty

carefully, lessons are laid
spread in sacred geometries before us
as resin clears the air of smoke
that *truly* obscures, that *incenses*
we honor all of the elements
liberations that cannot be contained
breathing in arcs of their design
each a consecrated sliver of tree
painted & blessed & teeming with epic quests
every color, every line, filled with symbology
only a true artist can render
heroes' journeys tenting principles universal
like the first tales taught us:

    "if you try to clench fire, your body will burn
    for freedom must dance earth
    on open palms"

    "hold cups steady as you walk with them
    for you might waste what could've nourished
    'stead of makin' a mess of yo' flo'"

    "point knives away from you
    but face them when passing to another
    without animosity"

    "careful how you wave that wand!
    alla we must access power, express desires, act on dreams
    careful you don't poke another's eye out! nor your own
    wands are intended to transcend, not blind"

AND

>"remember your values.
>carry them close; store them in your soul
>they hold major arcs, which bend
>far less frequently than nature"

pay attention to constructs
parting heritages that are found there
and coming legacies
cultures may shift with every (re)viewing
yet they are not simply transient
deeply rooted; they evolve
more slowly, perhaps, but
they evolve
interpretations mirror growth
our mindful experiences, our epiphanies
our enlightenments
are only as rooted as you or me
learn to evolve not at the pace
of wind dancing with flame
nor crashing waves, tides turning
like ground beneath our feet
but at the pace
of galaxies

this crystal clear
placed on this here altar
is a remnant of the North Star
may it refract soft light into rainbows
may it guide us to greater freedom
may it ever illuminate

now ~
let us

see

Prompt
by Sherese Francis

Symbols surround us everywhere we go. We can use symbols as portals to access our deepest memories. They help us see clearly the truths we need to guide us and help us remember what is significant in our lives. Write about the symbols and signs that show up in your life regularly. What meanings do they have for your life?

CODES

—

Define You?
by Zahura Akter

You are not a robot.
Do as you please.

       Let's play a video game.

No! You need to finish making food for the boys.
Clean the house, and take care of the family.

       But? You said I can do anything I want.
       I am not a robot!

Yes, but you are a girl.

       That is it! I am a girl. That's me.
          A girl.
       I am not a robot, yet I am a girl!

       SO, I am programmed
       to act a certain way.

Volumes down, high pitches not allowed.
Don't argue, be meek, don't compete with boys.
Nobody likes a girl like that in Bangladeshi culture.

       The code is—A Girl—it will reset, reprogram,
       reboot me to be a proper girl.
       Yet, I am not a robot.

I want to be a belly queen.
Glaze across the floor.
Catch every eye on my flawless steps.
But I am a religious girl, SO I have to hide my body from lustful eyes.
Centuries went by, yet you are a girl, the code didn't change.

Centuries, culture, cross-cultural, religion, and so on.
    What didn't touch me?
I crossed the Pacific Ocean. From saris, now in boots, jeans, and shirt,

YET! I am a girl.
The code of a girl didn't change.

    I am not a robot! BUT I am a girl¡

Prompt
by Sherese Francis

Girls are taught throughout various societies and cultures to hold themselves back and serve others instead of choosing their own desires. Write about the social rules you fight to affirm your humanity and define yourself for yourself. Create your own programming or code that affirms who you are.

Taboo Women
by Sherese Francis

No time for the boys who predate with their eyes, chase us around
to put rings on our fingers. What we want is the entire embrace
of history's memory around us. Not the placid prison of kinship,
not the hours spent in front of a stove reflecting the bitterness of kale.
Our destiny is not the dowry for the richness of other
lives. We will hold back the treasures for ourselves and
lock them from the boys who treat us as nothing more than a bedpot
to throw their desires into and to throw ours away. This is for the Black
women whose womanhood is always a question. This is for the Black
dahlias whose bodies are ripped apart and smiles are demanded. Hand
us back our voices instead, the mysteries of our bodies. We will take account,
the stories of our times. We will remember and speak our truths even with the knife
of silence threatened at our throats, even with the bullet ready to pierce the spine
of the lost bible of our heretical emotions. They are not enough to cure the appetite
of women whose names were hung, whose names were drowned everywhere.
We will pick their names and fill our bodies with their flow. We will make sacred
spaces where we were told not to go. We are no longer afraid to go.

Prompt
by Sherese Francis

Throughout much of our current history and socioreligious narratives, women have been told to give up their power to men and to find value in being valued by men instead of women seeing the value already in themselves. Write a piece that challenges the conventional and patriarchal stories and tales about women and about choosing to find value and power in what is taboo. Where are you no longer afraid to go?

Helping to Understand!
by Zahura Akter

He is your husband.
Do your duties to him.
He can do what he pleases.
You need to learn to be okay with it.
It's your fault when he goes to another.
Stop complaining. Stop crying.
 Bite your tongue. Honor your tradition.

I'm his wife!
Wearing high heels, tank top, glass in hand, and mingling with men.
I look across the room, see him bleed.
Now, you understand how you made me feel.
I am your wife! Doing my duties now, as I please.

Prompt

by Sherese Francis

Write a piece in which you decode between traditional social rules and the desires for your own self. In what ways do you choose to break away to do as you please or to show others what you want them to understand?

When I Come Back
by .CHISARAOKWU.

      I want to be woman
in another language
another way to beauty
without a man's tongue

      I want my name
unpronounceable
by misogynists & pedophiles
to taste like honeysuckle & lilac
to would-be lovers

      I want my body to be
an *un*birthing
a reverse hysteria
where my nulliparous womb does not
etch my epitaph

      Let my uterus be worn
across my torso like a satchel & be
filled with fairy dust & apples
that men with little hands eat
then choke on

      Let me be a *woo*
who origamis herself
into phoenixes & fires up
whenever a cad tries her—
sprinkles him with fairy dust
so he can't mansplain his way
out of ash & dust like Adam did.

Prompt
by .CHISARAOKWU.

This poem was written in response to all the things that women deal with in society today—the expectations, the labels, the mis-identities, the oppression. So I asked myself, "What Do I Want To Be When I Come Back?" as a way to find out what it is I need to be right now. Because isn't that usually the case—the impossible dream is the reality we want now. In your poem-generating space, think about the dreams that you have labeled impossible. No matter how far-fetched, supernatural, implausible they seem right now. Maybe it's a dream about what you want to do in your career, or in life, something from your childhood, or maybe you're a futurist like me, daring to reimagine a whole world that is equitable, or just plain different from the crazy that we have seen over the last several hundred years. Take some time to explore the impossible, no matter how scary or far-fetched. If you'd like, take what you write and add an anaphoric phrase to each stanza (e.g., the poem's first three stanzas begin with "I want"). Switch it up with each stanza. Are there spiritual elements, mystical elements, that you want to include? Whatever it is, make it yours– make your reimagined experience come alive on paper.

LETTERS

—

| after Lucille Clifton's "come celebrate with me" |
by blkcowrie

feed the soil
feed the soil

don't just show up for the teardown
and the turnup

feed the soil.

feed the soil
and watch things grow

      like your babies moving from you
          into this world   into new existences
  without you

      be fascinated   learn discover   *see*
finally, what happens when
we burn everything down

and begin again

    and ash turns to soil
    and you feed the soil
        and watch things grow

don't just burn things down

            feed the soil
                turn ash into earth

             into flower into tree
              into you into me

    feed the soil
and watch things grow

         move beyond fire.

                            reach water

Prompt
by Sherese Francis

Letters can be seen as seeds of thoughts we pass onto others. Whether we garden or communicate with letters, we are nurturing and growing a relationship. Write about "feeding the soil" in your life to grow "beyond fire." What is the water you are trying to reach? What new discoveries are you hoping to make when you let the old world burn away? What words of affirmation would you repeat to establish a cycle of nature within you and to grow relationships with others?

Relay Racing
by Kim D. Brandon

This is not a marathon, child
It is a relay
 A relay race

And when the stone-steel threads of love
Lay idol in the mud
The copper brown of rust making
Rings on what little love remained
After some heartache
That broke off a
Porous piece of family

Long before you arrived
There was a break in the love
That carried babies on backs
And bodies that worked that man's land

Long before you arrived
The love was thinned out like soup for unexpected company
Always a place for one more

Running over poverty and despair
The baton was passed hand- to-mouth
Dropped, rolled, even dragged into an uncertain future at times

Long before crack mamas arrived
There was love
Long before lynching, Jim Crow, and paddy wagons
There was love
and prison profits fatter than hog butts
The baton waited to be passed

And you see it there
In the unsung victories
The nameless kin
The disconnected stitch of rotgut, whiskey, and white lightnin'

Your fingers fold around the baton
And you run your leg of the race
Knowing that someone will be waiting
To carry the baton into the future

Their leg of the race
Even bloodier than yours
Hands up —don't shoot
Militarized policing
Will there be tanks on our streets?

Know of a champion's courage
And the cost of losing face
They eagerly await your baton pass
Low and steady
Swift and easy like air

Long after you are gone
They will write poems about the baton toss
They will include you and your sacrifices
And say words like
I stand in the shadow of giants
Who looked toward the future
Who ripped open a path for us to follow
Into the power of liberty.

Long after you are gone
There will be poems about the cost of you passing the baton
And the threadbare love that was recycled into your legacy

Pass…

Prompt
by Sherese Francis

Write about the legacies you hope to pass on to others. Where have legacies been dropped that you need to pick up and carry forward to the next part of the journey? How are you, as Veronica Agard says, an "ancestor in training"?

What I Leave Behind?
by Jacqueline Carr

What I leave behind?

I leave behind everything material

all my baggage, both physical and mental

real and imagined

my unsolved problems

my written works

my life lessons

my knowledge and the knowledge I imparted to others

What I leave behind?

Friendship that can never be bought, sold, or replaced

Family—their love, morals, and values

Unanswered questions

and **EVERYTHING**

that I can't physically and mentally take with me.

Prompt
by Sherese Francis

Letting go can be difficult to do. But letting go can open us up to the next stories and opportunities for our lives. We are reborn in letting go. What are you leaving behind? Write a list of the things you are deciding to let go.

What Would I Take?
by Jacqueline Carr

What would I take on my journey?

Absolutely NOTHING

It's a solo journey

for which I have no control

It would be taken empty-handed

without load,

and with some clothing that I once owned –

all my dreams, my ambitions,

my professional designations,

my quiet thoughts,

my unwhispered words encapsulated within my soul

What would I take on my journey?

Me, myself, and my soul

 All three of us **alone!**

Prompt
by Sherese Francis

Receptivity opens us up for many possibilities. It shows us the multitude of who we are. Write about how you are a receptacle and what you are receiving on your personal journeys.

Finding My Way
by LeConté Dill

> *She is warm wide and long.*
> *She laughs and she lingers.*
> —Gwendolyn Brooks, "My Grandmother Is Waiting for Me to Come Home"

I go back to her birthplace. She
left there long ago. Left us long ago. She is
from winding red clay roads and warm
greetings and *who your people is* and wide
porches and
I wander. Look for clues. I long.
I wonder about her mother and her mother and who my people is. She
is unmappable. Was unflappable. Her laughs
still visit me and
I listen, think she
magic. Hope hope lingers.

Prompt
by LeConté Dill

"Finding My Way" is a Golden Shovel poem. This poetic form was created by Terrance Hayes in 2010 in homage to Gwendolyn Brooks. "The Golden Shovel" is the name of the pool hall where Brooks's iconic poem "We Real Cool" is set. The last words of each line in a Golden Shovel poem are, in order, words from a line or phrase taken from a Brooks poem.

Write a Golden Shovel poem. Borrow a line or phrase from Brooks or another artist and use each of their words as the end-words in your new poem. Your new poem does not have to be about the same topic as the poem that offers the end-words. You can borrow from another poem, song, novel, play, speech, or film –just be sure to keep the original order of the words intact and give credit to the author of the original line or phrase.

Poor Dear
by Keisha-Gaye Anderson

Poor dear

You followed a firefly question
down a ditch
into the dark
looking for a truth
a way to untangle
a why
stampeding through time
an avalanche of poison
turning all your names
to ash

And you landed in a world of illusion
solidity cemented by collective confusion
and the noisy madness
of breathing bodies
stacking bricks
to hoard life

All the plants
the rivers
the clouds gliding by
are the same swirling song

A dream we play
and forget
we are weaving
from the inside
out of solutions for seeing
our own faces
we keep chasing a tale

And forget
that we should just laugh
at the shape of it
all

Follow the doors
to the end of the
maze

Stay awake
long enough
never to fall
again

Prompt
by Sherese Francis

Write a letter to yourself about the journey of arriving here to this place. What questions did you follow? What lessons have you learned on this journey that you want others to know?

Acknowledgements

— "When I Come Back" by .CHISARAOKWU. was first published in *Amistad's* Spring 2021 issue.

— "Homily on High" and "Mettle," both by Carla Cherry, were first published in issue 1 of *Variety Pack*.

— "Poor Dear" by Kiesha-Gaye Anderson was published in Anderson's book *A Spell for Living*.

— 1 Quote in introduction is from page 201 of *Beloved*.

Bios

.CHISARAOKWU., MD is an X-disciplinary poet artist, actor, and healthcare futurist based in the US. A first-generation Igbo in America, her artistic practice is inspired by the spiritual, oral, and print archives of the Igbo and her work as a physician and trauma specialist. Her art has been supported with grants, fellowships, and residencies from MacDowell, the California Arts Council, Headlands Center for the Arts, Cave Canem, Anaphora Arts, Tin House, Banff Centre for Arts and Creativity, the Vermont Studio Center, and more. She facilitates healing and arts workshops through her platform called The JOY+WELL which centers the works and experiences of women of the African diaspora. A poetry reader for *The Rumpus,* her work appears or is forthcoming in *Hayden's Ferry Review, Indiana Review, Transition, Obsidian,* and *The New England Journal of Medicine,* and more. She is an alum of Stanford University, Duke University School of Medicine, and UNC Gillings School of Global Health. Find more of her work at www.chisaraokwu.com.

Zahura Akter grew up in New York City, between Bengali and American cultures. She graduated from the City College of New York with a master's degree. Her first poetry book is *Traditional Paradox* from Banglar Kobita Prokashon. Her poetry has appeared in *Poetry in Performance, Free Verse,* and *Harlequin Creature.* Her writing is about ordinary people who have extraordinary qualities within them.

Keisha-Gaye Anderson is a Jamaican-born poet, author, and visual artist based in Brooklyn whose books include *Everything Is Necessary* (Willow Books), *Gathering the Waters* (Jamii Publishing), and *A Spell for Living* (Agape Editions), which was Editor's Choice for Agape's Numinous Orisons, Luminous Origin Literary Award. Her poetry, fiction, and essays have been widely published in national literary journals, magazines, and anthologies that include *Kweli Journal, Small Axe Salon, Interviewing the Caribbean, Renaissance Noire, The Caribbean Writer, The Killens Review of Arts and Letters, Mosaic Literary Magazine, African Voices Magazine, The Langston Hughes Review, Streetnotes: Cross-Cultural Poetics, Caribbean in Transit Arts Journal, The Mom Egg Review,* and others. She is a past participant of the VONA Voices and Callaloo writing workshops and was shortlisted for the Small Axe Literary Award. Her visual art has been featured in numerous exhibitions and in such literary journals such as *The Adirondack Review, Joint Literary Magazine, MER VOX, Culture Push,* and *No, Dear Magazine*. In 2018, Keisha was selected as a Brooklyn Public Library Artist in Residence. In 2021, she was presented with the Poetic Icon Award by her alma mater, Syracuse University. Keisha holds an MFA in fiction from the City College, CUNY. Learn more about Keisha's published works and art at www.keishagaye.ink.

blkcowrie is a butterfly mermaid scribe who seeks to foment beauty, cultivate collective empathy, and conjure we/i&i anew. From soaring cosmic contemplations to engaging frontlines of revolutionary community struggles to navigating permeability, love, pain, and healing of the self, blkcowrie and her pen move to the music of water & flowers as she wanders & wonders at the soul's journey. Published twice in *ESSENCE* magazine as a young teen, her poems appear in *Lucky Jefferson, Apogee Journal,* and Gallery Aferro's inaugural *Poem Booth,* among others. A member of the Choir of Imagineers, blkcowrie is creatress of the grassroots marketing challenge #UbuntuPoetryPortal celebrating low-resourced, conscious, and emerging poets of color. blkcowrie is a Writing Fellow for *The Watering Hole*. (she/her/us/we/sweetness) @blkcowrie https://linktr.ee/blkcowrie

Kim D. Brandon is a poet/artist/activist/storyteller. Her work has been included in *50IN50: Letters to Our Daughters,* which was performed at the Kumble Theater in Brooklyn and the Waco Theater in Los Angles in March 2019. She also appears in *50IN50: What Place Do We Have in This Movement?* which was performed at the Billie Holiday Theater in spring 2018. Kim has been published in *The Dream Catcher's Song,* an anthology of five emerging Brooklyn women writers in 2009, *Boundaries and Borders,* an anthology of Women of Color Writers (fall 2019), *the Hawaii Review* (2016), the *Peregrine Journal* (2016, 2018, 2019). She has been the featured poet/artist at numerous events, workshops, and civil rights rallies and has been a featured storyteller in schools and cultural events. In 2018, Kim was presented with a citation for community service from the Brooklyn Borough President, Eric Adams. She was featured in the American Ethical Union's 2019 publication, *Ethical Humanist.*

Jacqueline Carr is a literary enthusiast, a community advocate, a published author, and a poet. She is the holder of the Distinguished Toastmaster (DTM) award and formerly worked as an adjunct lecturer at York College of the City University of New York (CUNY). In September of 2019, Ms. Carr was presented with a City Council Citation for community service from Council Member Rory I. Latchman. She was also presented with a New York State Assembly Citation in July 2017 for exemplary service to her community from Clyde Vanel, Member of Assembly. Ms. Carr has written three books of poems. The titles of her three books are: *Hands of Time, Quiet Thoughts,* and *A Selected Few Just For You.* The collection, *A Selected Few Just For You,* is an easy read, age appropriate, inspirational, and insightful. The language usage is simplistic in its profundity. Some of her poems will give you cause for pause; some will make you smile, while others are thought-provoking in their analogies. Ms. Carr can be reached at minelvas@aol.com. Her website is www.minelvas.wixsite.com/jackie

Carla M. Cherry is an English teacher and poet. Her work has appeared in various publications, including *Random Sample Review, Eunoia Review, MemoryHouse,* and *Raising Mothers.* She is the author of six books of poetry, *Gnat Feathers and Butterfly Wings, Thirty Dollars and a Bowl of Soup, Honeysuckle Me, These Pearls Are Real, Stardust and Skin,* and *May He Bless My Name* (iiPublishing), and two chapbooks: *Clap Your Hands, Stomp Your Feet* (Grandma Moses Press) and *Sundays and Hot Buttered Rolls: A Granddaughter of Harlem Speaks* (Finishing Line Press). Carla holds a Master of Fine Arts in Creative Writing from the City College of New York.

LeConté Dill is a writer, scholar, and educator from South Central Los Angeles. She holds degrees from Spelman College, UCLA, and UC Berkeley, has participated in VONA Voices and Cave Canem writing workshops, and has been a Callaloo and Huston/Wright Fellow. She is an Associate Professor of African American and African Studies at Michigan State University. Her work has been published in spaces such as *Poetry Magazine, Killens Review of Arts & Letters, Mom Egg Review,* and *The Feminist Wire.*

Sherese Francis describes themselves as an Alkymist of the I-Magination, finding expression through poetry, interdisciplinary arts, workshop facilitation, editing, and literary curation. Her(e) work takes inspiration from her(e) Afro-Caribbean heritage (Barbados and Dominica), and studies in Afrofuturism and Black Speculative Arts, mythology, and etymology. Some of their work has been published in *Furious Flower, Obsidian, Rootwork Journal, The Caribbean Writer, The Operating System, Cosmonauts Avenue, No Dear, Apex Magazine, Bone Bouquet, African Voices, Newtown Literary,* and *Free Verse.* Additionally, Sherese has published four chapbooks, *Lucy's Bone Scrolls* (Three-Legged Elephant, 2017), *Variations on Sett/ling Seed/ling* (Harlequin Creature, 2018), *Recycling a Why That Rules Over My Sacred Sight* (DoubleCross Press, 2021) and *Lady Liberty Smashing Stones* (THRASH Press, 2022). Sherese was a finalist for the Furious Flower poetry prize (2020) and CAAPP Book Prize (2021) and won The Caribbean Writer's Vincent Cooper Literary Prize (2021) for the poem, "SomNuh/Mbulist (Patois Possession)."

Jacqueline Johnson is a multi-disciplined artist creating in both poetry, fiction writing and fiber arts. She is the author of *A Woman's Season* (Main Street Rag Press) and *A Gathering of Mother Tongues* (White Pine Press) and is the winner of the Third Annual White Pine Press Poetry Award. Her work has appeared in *This is the Honey: An Anthology of Contemporary Black Poets,* edited by Kwame Alexander (Little Brown, February 2024); *About Place Journal,* an online journal; and *Revisiting the Elegy in the Black Lives Matter Era* (Routledge 2020). She is a Cave Canem fellow and Black Earth Institute Senior Fellow. Works in progress include: *Golden Lady,* a poetry manuscript *The Privilege of Memory,* a novel, and *How to Stop a Hurricane,* a collection of short stories. A native of Philadelphia, PA., she resides in Brooklyn, New York.

Divya Kandwal currently lives in India and is an amateur baker and an aspiring gardener. She believes that all of life's answers can be found within the folds of books. Somehow a cat lady without a cat, she cares deeply about issues of gender, race, and social justice. She loves long walks, dark overcast skies, and Nina Simone. She maintains that a flower growing through a crack in a pavement is one of the bravest things she has ever seen.

Kuukua Dzigbordi Yomekpe is a transdisciplinary artist, choreographing West African dance forms, creating a fusion of Ghanaian dishes, and penning memoirs, essays, and social commentaries. She is the author of several essays and prose poems, some of which have been included in *Berkshire Mosaic, Writing Fire: An Anthology Celebrating the Power of Women's Words, Pentimento, Fierce Hunger: Writing From the Intersection of Trauma and Desire, African Women Writing Resistance, Becoming Bi: Bisexual Voices from Around the World,* and *Inside Your Ear.* Her master's thesis, "The Audacity to Remain Single: Single Black Women in the Black Church," is anthologized in *Queer Religion II* (Praeger Publishers). She's also contributed to several blogs: *The Feminist Wire, Queermentalhealth.org, This Is Africa, Digging Through The Fat, Spoonwiz,* and *Hola Africa.*

www.ingramcontent.com/pod-product-compliance
Lightning Source LLC
LaVergne TN
LVHW072132060526
838201LV00072B/5016